Mata Hari Blows a Kiss

Lisa Dominguez Abraham

Swan Scythe Press

ISBN 978-1-930454-45-3

Swan Scythe Press
1468 Mallard Way
Sunnyvale, CA 94087
www.swanscythe.com

Editor: Robert S. Pesich
Founding Editor: Sandra McPherson
Book Design, Production & *Cover Design*: Mark Deamer and Andrew Rivera Shannon
Cover Art: "La Gran Venus", 1979 by Ricardo Martínez (1918-2009)
    Oil on canvas
    210 x 175 cm
    Tlatelolco Cultural Center, National Autonomous University of Mexico

Swan Scythe Press thanks Fundación Ricardo Martínez de Hoyos AC for their generous
    permission to reproduce "La Gran Venus".

Swan Scythe Press books are distributed by
    Small Press Distribution, http://www.spdbooks.org

Printed in the United States of America.

Mata Hari Blows a Kiss

CONTENTS

For my sisters

God Poured Voice

God poured voice in me, a woman-shaped bowl,
then skimmed a finger along the rim

until I hummed. I was set down,
a bowl of breath and space in Eden's green

and though Adam's skin at daybreak glowed
like home, I couldn't rest, and restless

sought the apple tree, blossoms unfolding
into fruit, the apples kin to stars

speeding from Big Bang. I hungered for surge,
a straight shot to the unknown

and bit through, juice bathing my vocal cords,
my voice no longer God's alone.

The Axial Tilt of Earth

Like everyone, I follow directives below recognition
until I arrive in a roomful of strangers

who have dyed their hair
and carefully shopped for workout pants,

a room where the metallic fragrance
of hand weights expands behind my eyes

and scent becomes sound. The air rings
with Beyoncé's affirmations as I watch myself repeat

lifts in time with the other women,
apparently solid though I'm pierced

by texts and calls through each cell.
This is how I live most days, unaware

of solar wind and the earth's axial tilt.
Our teacher is grey-haired

and strong. She nods to the music,
shows us how rhythm increases

the body's telepathy until we move in synch.
And though each woman arrived separately,

together we face the huge gym mirror,
lifting and lowering outstretched arms.

Newlywed

Alone in an ice house tidied with wallpaper
and rented cheap off-season,
I imagined the former tenants: ice blocks.

For hours I studied Betty Crocker's
gingham-print cookbook and practiced
waiting for my husband

by brushing sand and more sand
off the mattress. Through afternoons
I walked empty streets

keen to spy behind closed curtains
the sextants and compasses
nailed to walls, reduced to relic

as sea wind scoured porches and eaves.
I was nineteen and didn't know artists
begin in places like this.

Emigration

Last week I scrubbed yellow shadows
from my bedroom wall, erasing
the last traces of wedding pictures
carefully stored away.

For a moment, emptiness felt clean.
But each night as my children
turn through sleep, I dream:

I am my grandmother raising a lantern
as she crosses a stubble field in Zacatecas
to bargain with a ghost for silver.
It's 1914. Soldiers have slaughtered
all her chickens, sliced the corn field with bayonets.
Her daughters shiver in the barn and I'm frightened
feeling my legs in her skirts
until courage contracts
to a metallic taste on my tongue.
Coiled around a filthy sack
in a shallow cave, the ghost lets me
grab one handful of silver

and I wake gripping my own thumbs.
Guitarróns thrum from the clock radio.
On folded newspapers, three paint cans.

I'll pry open the lids,
stir lilac, white and green,
then paint my walls with pictographs—
a band of women traveling
toward a country they've never seen.

True Love

When I met his enlightened eyes
and stroked his finely-sanded

wooden belly painted leaf-green,
I sensed a frog-shaped hole in my torso

empty all my life. Now my *alebrije*
perches on my nightstand

and I no longer fear the descent
into dream. His amphibian smile leads me

across the reed bridge strung over
a river gorge. I trust my dream feet

on slick rope because he knows water
and grip. His back is speckled

like cottonwood duff alighting on ponds
and like all mystery

is multi-hued so I can spot him
even in murky water as he leads me

through shallows and reeds up the path
to a hole in willow bark, a nest

where I curl, slow my breath,
my heartbeat, awaiting the new.

Return: Sunday Morning in Watts

There's the yard where Mom threw feed
to fierce *pollitos* raised to fight as cocks,
mad puffs, quick beaks that pecked her feet.

And from the bright pink house, *rancheras* trumpet
like they did when Rosa's 'uncles' visited
one hour at a time after church.

Mom takes my arm and we enter church,
the Mass still said in Spanish, the same grim saints,
El Señor a manikin, his beard glued on imperfectly.

From church we stroll to her old school and she returns
the smiles of everyone, a woman in a hair net,
a junkie pedaling by. For once

an ocean breeze slips through the factories
that loom around this neighborhood.
Mom watches the playground's poplar trees

shimmy and inhales the air
that smells just as she remembers, warm
and spiced with salt and balsam.

Hoodoos Will Appear Where You Are Standing

The ground feels solid as my own rib cage pressing into the rail that keeps me from the drop into Bryce Canyon. An information panel describes what will be here in the future—more sandstone spires as the canyon widens. I thought hoodoo meant the power to charm or curse, but here it testifies to what lasts.

From my mother's core,
though memory crumbles, her
laugh is strong and clear

Stone Soup

I.   *Arturo in Watts*

The pond was still until I dropped lettuce and earthworms on its surface.
Then koi rose, glittering like Kazuko's tiara when she waved from a pick-up
festooned with flowers, the Strawberry Queen. I was the scrawny boy she didn't
notice in the crowd. Two weeks later a military truck hauled her family to
Manzanar. I wanted her to return to find her fish grown, each scale magnified,
more brilliant than she remembered. I wanted her to know what the powerless
can do for one another.

II.   *Kazuko in San Francisco*

My first job after camp was in an office high rise. I could see down into the
piano store where Dad bought the upright we had to leave behind. My boss
left loose diamonds scattered across his desk. He would pick one at random,
absently rub numbers tattooed on his forearm as he lost himself in the gem
scope's enlargement of angular facts. He wanted hot coffee, a secretary who
hungered more for Mozart than for stones. Each week I cashed my paycheck,
dropped dollars into a jar hidden behind my icebox. When they reached the
rim, I bought a used piano.

III.   *Stone on a desk*

I've been prised from settings,
sewn into coat linings
time and again. Beneath anxiety
each owner brings what she's kept hidden
among the carrots and potatoes
of her dreams. Her eye
makes me a pool
to cast a wish into.
My clarity isn't emptiness.
I flicker with light.

Jack and the Beanstalk

She won't apologize for shouting
but packs a lunch for his climb

then waits below to throw him an ax,
shocked by the giant who falls and flattens

their wheat field. Second shock: Giant's blood
plumps the wheat kernels

she harvests and grinds for daily bread
that's darker, more moist than before.

At each meal she studies her boy.
No longer starved, he grows taller

and each day more inclined
to gaze past her. Jack studies

the clouds as he chews, sotto voce
humming the songs he heard among them.

Christmas Concert

The parents enter exhausted, ears ringing
with the evening commute, with radio news

of bombs in Kabul and campus gunfire
one town over. Even among sparkly cardboard bells

each thinks ahead to a fast food dinner
then bills, then laundry.

Then the curtain stutters open. A third-grader
runs to the piano, arches his hands and plays

Pachelbel's canon in D, notes chosen over 300 years ago
still true. The adults shift and raise eyebrows—

surprisingly good—he's like their own kids, noticed
mostly in fed-up swats and after-bath cuddle.

When did he learn to wait for end notes
to fade into prayer?

Next, a chubby, messy girl walks onstage.
Mid-December, she wears navy-blue shorts

bunched at the crotch and stares at some back corner
to focus, to project her voice in tones so pure

adult smirks freeze. Somewhere outside
the stars are brightly shining

and the audience stills, listening
as she sings a nearly forgotten secret,

as though she is the winter secret
whose breath exhales promise.

The Iron Goddess of Mercy

sees herself in the child hiding
between a mattress and box springs

as his mother smacks her belt against the wall
and screams what she'll do if she finds him.

The goddess finds her own small face
weighted, breathing dust

and sends him a faint note
of honeysuckle. He can sense it

eyes clenched. Years after his escape
he will plant that tangled vine

to remind himself of hope. And decades later
the goddess, being iron

will allow her face to bend into
the mother's pinched expression

unfocused now. She will grant her
a cup of pale green tea

a hint of honey and herb. And because the mother
has lost touch with everyone

she tried to care for, has lost even her rage,
the goddess will allow her to forget.

Weeding the Cosmos

I read myself into picture books of myth,
a woman who spins cloth and hunts wild boar,
until the day my body broke open
in childbirth. One week later I curled on my side

nursing our newborn while my husband
rubbed himself against my haunches.
Then I saw myself as an instrument
for others, my skin a balloon
for silence.

My story should turn here,
the woman gathers herself, speaks up,
but in that moment I sensed
my original sisters across the globe—
one in Uruguay, another in Burundi—
each one rubbing a husband's shoulders,
braiding a daughter's hair,
dreaming herself in a story where a woman
hikes alone through wilderness
armed with her folktales.

I try to meet their hard acceptance
of what's real. I've grown into a woman
who can chop down jasmine with no remorse
though it's scented like a princess.
Its woody stem will be shredded,
turned into the soil, just as
my own body still has its uses.

Like women everywhere, I tend the growing
and the dying. Shovel in hand,
kneeling among spindly flowers
I know *woman* as constellation,
the base of my spine one star,
the crown of my head another,
a gardener weeding the cosmos.

Blow a Kiss

I.   *Mata Hari*

Men smoke in safe shadows,
Watch the hypnotic drop of veils

until my oiled hips and V of hair
glow in plain sight,
the secret they want most

revealed. Outside they long for
the courage to air each treasure
they've been given.

Here they inhale
the scents of another country,
imagine a culture

where each truth is shared.
Palms up, I welcome them in.

II.   *The German Officer*

My chest constricts in staff meetings
where facts choke my lungs.

Even at home when I taste
the brine and frill of my wife,
the moment passes too quickly.

I long for an exhale, for secrets
to swirl out past my teeth

Jonah through the whale's mouth
back into the sea.

III. *The French Soldier*

Rifle raised, I aim for her heart,
but just before she's blindfolded

she spots me, knows
I'm like the others, a man

who longs for the slip and heat
of bodies.

My commander gives the count
and she whisks off her blindfold,

blows me a kiss. When my bullets
open her chest, she stains the wall

and looks as though
she could be any of us.

Passing Through

I pull sheets from the queen in 303,
stoop for booze bottles and collapsed condoms—

we're not so ephemeral as some suppose.
Each day new guests delight

in taut sheets and little soaps,
this room a shimmer that will burst

forgotten upon check out
along with all they leave behind—magic

in pared nails and stray hairs.
I'm here to sweep up and disinfect

the proof of lives passing through.
It's what they pay for, luggage gleaming

on stiff leashes they pull down the hall
as though there's no trail

of footprints in the carpet, no thumbprint
pressed in bathroom counter shine.

Blue Corn Woman

(Based on a Huíchol myth)

She slept by her sisters, Red Corn and Yellow Corn,
their dreams knotting into corn cobs they gave away
to polite ants, needy sparrows. Each day they played dress-up
and she fell for make-believe like every girl—
someday she'd have a husband, her cheek in the curve
between his shoulder and chest, like heaven, that myth
of both arrival and rest. But her mother sent her away
to save the village of Colotlán where children suffered
distended bellies and stick arms, sent her with a starving man
disguised as his bride.

Her mother warned her to keep it simple, to sit alone
each day gathering strength for sleep, to lay alone
each night so her dreams could bead into kernels—
violet, cream and inky black, a pile of cobs in the *zócolo*
the village would bless, a miracle. But from within her hut
she could hear other women call her the lazy girl,
too stuck-up to work. That's why, impatient and lonely,
she tried to prove herself with a wife's task—
pat masa into a tortilla, set it on the *comal*.

She forgot that her skin, being corn, would blister along fingertips,
up her arms. Her husband found her curled and burned,
human now. He let her stay until she healed
with crumpled skin that keeps sweat from trickling out
or dreams from seeping in. Now in Mazatlán she lives on a sidewalk
and twists together shoulder bags for tourists
as she strains each morning to hear her sisters' dreams—
from distant hills the rumble of red and yellow corn.
Even on a crowded street she hears silk tassels hiss.
She knows it's her sisters who send the breeze
that ruffles her hair, cools her cheek.

Toshiko Takaezu's Closed Mouth Vase

If there's an accident—the vase shatters—
three or four shards will reveal words

scored with a stylus before Takaezu
pinched the mouth closed.

One might read *core*,
a fragment in the alluvial scatter.

The artist, a woman of these times,
thought ahead. She reminds the stricken owner

that even an irreplaceable world
offers tidings from the wet clay of its creation

hidden until the old form breaks open.

Breadcrumbs

Not birds but a sculptor has gathered
Hansel and Gretel's dropped bread crumbs

and glued them into a tiny loaf of bread
strategically lit to glisten

as an art installation. He's also built
a drum kit from the towel-wrapped water jug

a teenager dropped as she made her way north
through dust and scorpions.

Art aficionados walk around the kit,
study an unknown girl's despair.

Some sense she makes it from Sinaloa
where teenagers wield guns

all the way to the candied land where she
sorts grapes for artists who make wine.

It's unclear which side of the border
is home or oven

as she stands beside other masked women,
quick hands working to send

whatever she can
from a thin paycheck south.

Grown and Gone

I wash the walls of this quirky home
like women wash gravestones, tending
the presence of loved ones

they no longer touch. Fingerprints fade
while I daydream a narrow forest behind the plaster,
all wooden frame and frizzy electric wire.

Outside these walls in distant cities
my sons live their own elliptical paths
around the sun. Electricity threads

from their heads to mine. Quiet mostly
and then a spark. They're vibrant
as the Chinese pistache outside the window

flickering yellows and reds. Autumn
shines the room, almost liquid,
and rinses the silence alive.

The Lost Woman of San Nicolas

No one saw me slip over the rail
until I was already swimming home
to save myself from missionaries
who planned to save our tribe.
Wave-slapped, I saw the ship
tack toward the mainland, my parents
shrieking as I disappeared from view.

Eighteen years later, I stand on another ship
watching my whalebone fence shrink
to a white dot on the bluff.
For weeks I hoisted ribs up from the beach
to plant in a semi-circle before my cave,
points curving outward.
Onto them I carved my effigies.
Women scraping otter skins, laughing
and slyly judging each other.
Men posturing by fire
or seated, chipping obsidian
into spear points.

Often wild dogs skulked and growled
outside my fence. But within
my inside-out whale, I could consider
what I needed to be:
a man-spirit who fashioned tools, hunted.
A woman who used sinew to stitch
cormorant feathers into a cape
becoming sometimes the bird itself—
draped in feathers I'd pace the cliffs,
peering out to sea.

When I spot this ship, it simply means
a transition. I'm ready to go now.
My family so long imagined
brush the air by my shoulders.
I'll be taken, as they were, to missionaries
who will offer me a dusty courtyard
to sweep each morning and give me
tuberculosis. The mission padre will record

that I was the last speaker of my language
and never learned his.

Why bother?
Father Gonzales has no words
for who I am on this day
before he clothes me as one of his own.
My island reduced to a smear on the horizon,
I lean against a cold brass rail.
Breasts bare for the last time,
my cape flutters and shakes
back to the wheeling sea birds
iridescent wings.

Las Brujas

For Q

You see us first as lit candles,
as flickers nestled in red roses
we pinned in our hair,
then by the wavering glow
of white lace shawls, our full lace skirts
held out like fans. We turn a slow circle,
our skirts brushing one another,
dancing, candles balanced on our heads
at two in the morning.
Syncopated heel beats
draw you to us,
seven candles below
the expansive night sky,
below where you watch
our sparks rising
as you flicker high above.

Flounder: On Turning Fifty

I loved my old look, a transparent fry
swaying with the current until
a slow intestinal twist, muscle net
pulling my right eye toward the left.

Now seawater feels too loose.
Now safety means nestling
in sand, just my eyes above the silt.
Here I watch the downward drift,

kelp bits and dropped mouthfuls,
watch the typical fish parade and flick
above the bed where I sense something
larger than the sea. Light spreads far above

and below my fins, the allure of gravity.
I flatten into the subliminal. My skeleton hosts
murmurs that swirl and school. I dream
syllables, then words unhitching each bone.

Donne's Compass

"Thy firmness makes my circle just
And makes me end where I begun."
— *John Donne*

It's go time. Your dust-coated Peterbilt
edges from the chute as cattle shoulder
one another and low, settling in for
the ride. Fighting sleep, you call me

to talk, keep you crisp. On the old paper
map I keep open the weeks you're gone, I
find the highway town where you fuel, a dot
on a line, and from there trace the back roads

around Wyoming scales, imagining
your stops at ranches and feedlots. Our cell
phones are miracles. My voice reaches through
your exhaustion until you say your eyes

can focus. The road is clear and you can
picture it now, our kitchen table, home.

Acknowledgments

Cumberland River Review	Christmas Concert
Moibus	Stone Soup
North American Review	Grown and Gone
Prairie Schooner	Emigration* The Lost Woman of San Nicolas*
Southern Review	Jack and the Beanstalk
Sow's Ear Poetry Review	Flounder: On Turning Fifty
Tertulia Magazine	Passing Through

(*These poems were published in slightly different versions under my former married name.)